Phillip Newell _____ Tasmania, an island diocese, since 1982. He likes to remind people that, dating from 1842, Tasmania is Australia's oldest diocese. He is also the Anglican Church of Australia's episcopal representative on the Anglican Consultative Council, and Chair of the General Board of Religious Education, the national church's education body. With his wife Merle, he has served in parish ministry in Melbourne, Sydney and Brisbane. They have three adult sons. Bishop Phillip Newell began his working life as a teacher of mathematics and physics, having graduated in science and education from the University of Melbourne. He later returned to the University to study theology and complete a post-graduate degree in education.

The Pocket Lent Book

PHILLIP NEWELL

TRI△NGLE

First published under the title *Body Search*
in Australia in 1994 by
AIO Press, Australia

First published in Great Britain in 1996 by
Triangle
SPCK
Holy Trinity Church
Marylebone Road
London NW1 4DU

All scripture quotations are taken from
The New Revised Standard Version
of the Bible © 1989, and The
Revised Standard Version of the Bible
© 1971 and 1952.

British Library Cataloguing-in-Publication Data
A catalogue record for this book is available from the British
Library
ISBN 0-281 04917–3

Typeset by Dorwyn Ltd, Rowlands Castle, Hants

Printed in Great Britain by BPC paperbacks Ltd

CONTENTS

For Merle

FOREWORD

Of the making of Lent books there seems to be no end. However, I welcome this one because of the freshness of its approach. Bishop Phillip Newell bids us look at our bodies — hands, feet, eyes, tongues, ears — and allow them to teach us the lessons which our Creator-God has built into them. The Bishop is not the first to do that by any means. Evelyn Underhill told us to look at an object — a candle, a leaf, a stone, a flower, our own hand — and focus simply and wholly on it; that way we might learn to meditate and to resolve. Dean Michael Mayne makes much of this approach in his recent book *This Sunrise of Wonder*. And anyone who has read *The Forever Feast* by Paul Brand, that insightful missionary doctor, will treat his body with greater reverence and awe than he did before that book came his way.

The Bishop, then, takes a time-honoured approach to devotion and handles it in an eminently practical way. The book is not for the advanced mystic. It comes from the pen of a man who has spent his life, as priest and bishop, in ministering to ordinary people in their needs — a man who believes with all his heart in the Incarnate Christ. Thus the book is securely earthed and keeps us close to Scripture.

A good Lent to all who read this book! They will not do so in vain.

Donald Coggan

INTRODUCTION

The purpose of this book is to offer the Church a series of reflections for use each day from Ash Wednesday to Easter Day.

Years ago, as a parish priest, I discovered that the children's addresses given during the Sunday service needed to be more than words. Some concrete illustration or object was called for. It was an approach which appealed to the teacher in me.

In *The Pocket Lent Book* I have tried to apply the same principle. One thing which we all have is a body. Some may lack one or two functions but most of us will be able to reflect on the significance of our hands, feet, eyes, tongues and ears. So for each week of Lent a different part of the human body is 'searched' for the meaning and message it may have for us. It is a simple approach and one which I hope will be useful to others. In a way it is sacramental. We start with the outward and visible members of the human body and we search to find what inward and spiritual meaning or message may be conveyed.

It will be necessary to set aside some time each day, say fifteen minutes. A quiet, contemplative location is preferable. The equipment required consists of yourself, a Bible, this book and perhaps paper and pencil. Begin with a period of quiet, settling into the presence of God. It may help to say, 'Be still and know that I am God', repeated if you like. Merge from words into stillness, into wordless silence, at least for a minute or two. Then I suggest a deliberate reading of the biblical reference at the top of each page. It is printed there for you.

If you can also open your Bible and find the verse, reading it in context, then so much the better.

Next comes the reflection using some aspect of the human body. Again, do not rush. Take it gently. Explore the topic for yourself. Let the printed reflection spark off your own response. Sometimes I have suggested questions. Answer them simply, directly and honestly. In one way, what I have written does not really matter very much. It is meant to be a catalyst, a start. Your own reflection is what is most important. Indeed, it may well turn out to be God's reflection for you. The reflection is followed by a short prayer and then a suggested resolution. The experience each day is to be valued for itself. But if it is to 'make a difference', then a resolution can be helpful.

At the end of each section there are some discussion questions. If the book is used by a group then these could form the basis for discussion at a weekly session.

Perhaps I should say one more thing about the use of Scripture. Sometimes the reflection is based quite specifically on the text. At other times I have left the reader to make and explore the connection.

If the members of our bodies have messages for us, then they are messages which we take with us every day.

I would like to thank Henry Porteous and Charlotte Rivers for their encouragement and Janet Koop, my secretary, for her typing of the manuscript.

Phillip Newell
Bishop of Tasmania

Our Hands

Clean Hands

Draw near to God, and he will draw near to you.
Cleanse your hands, you sinners, and purify your
hearts, you double-minded. (Jas. 4.8)

REFLECTION

'Wash your hands, Geoffrey! With soap, Geoffrey!'

We begin our Lenten exercises by looking at our hands, examining them, thinking, Where have my hands been? What have they been involved in? Our hands can tell us a lot about ourselves. So look at them carefully; you may see in them the story of your life. Where you have been, your hands have been.

So sit quietly for a time and look at your hands. Listen to what they are saying to you. What have they done? Are they honest hands, instruments of good, or do they tell a different story? There are the innocent hands of babies and the guilty hands of Pontius Pilate which, endlessly washed, never seem to come clean. Make a list of the things of which your hands accuse you. Own them before God. These are your hands, no one else's.

Now let your hands take you deeper into your life. The story of our hands is the outer reflection of the story of our hearts. It is there that the real trouble lies, sacramentally washed once in baptism, but spoiled in thought and word as well as in deed. You may need to add to your list.

But is this Lenten journey to be just another guilt trip? God forbid. The gospel is good news. It is about dirty hands washed clean and guilty hands made new. The forgiving love of God is always ready to wash over us and through us.

So, 'Draw near to God and he will draw near to you.' Imagine that you are placing your hands into a large basin of pure water. Actually go and do it if you want to. Immerse them, in imagination or in reality, in cool, clear water. That water represents the depth of God's love for you. He is washing you clean even as he is loving you.

'Wash me thoroughly from my iniquity, and cleanse me from my sin.' (Ps. 51.2) Look at your hands again. They are clean and it is God's doing. Tear up your list and dispose of it. It is finished with!

PRAYER
Loving Lord, I thank you for making me a member of the household of faith with all those who were baptized into your name. Help me to live in obedience to the promises made in my baptism; for Jesus' sake. (Adapted from *An Australian Prayer Book*.)

RESOLUTION
Each time I wash my hands today I will give thanks for the cleansing, freeing love of God.

Still Hands

Every day I call on you, O Lord; I spread out my hands to you. (Ps. 88.9)

REFLECTION

'For Satan finds some mischief still for idle hands to do.' (Isaac Watts)

There is a world of difference, however, between idle hands and still hands. One of the hardest things to do with our lives is to let them be still. The Psalmist wisely counsels, 'Be still and know that I am God.' But most of us are activists. Quietness frightens us.

As with our lives so with our hands. We find it hard to keep them still. So today may be a little difficult, at least to begin with. Yet if we are to be in tune with God we must at times still our hands, our lives, our lips. 'Be still and know that I am God.'

When we were little some of us were taught to put our hands together as we knelt at the bedside for our evening prayers. I can still remember being taught, as a young choir boy, how to put my hands together whilst seated or kneeling in the choir stalls.

The disposition to pray begins with empty hands, still hands. For, 'Nothing in my hand I bring, simply to thy cross I cling.'

Sit then or kneel with still hands, empty hands, joined hands. Be still and content in the presence of God. This is the starting point of all true prayer, personal or corporate. We need bring nothing except ourselves. We need do nothing except wait on him. Be still. God is great. God is good. God is present.

After a few minutes of stillness, use your hands in a different way. It is the way suggested in today's biblical text. It is another way of coming to God with still hands. Open your hands a little and turn the palms upwards. Yes, they are still hands and empty hands but now they are open, waiting, receptive. God is not only great and good and present, he loves you. He seeks you. He is always moving towards you. Your receptive hands are an invitation which he gladly accepts. Your outstretched hands like your waiting heart are his point of entry. 'Every day I call on you, O Lord; I spread out my hands to you.' Spend a little time in this posture, soaking up, breathing in, absorbing the love and power of the Divine Presence. Our hands can teach us a simple approach to prayer.

PRAYER
Dear God, deliver me from that ceaseless busyness which keeps you at a distance. Still my hands and empty them; still my heart and empty it of all that is not of you. Then, as I wait, come quietly to claim me as your own. May my waiting hands be your entry point to my waiting heart. Even so, come, Lord Jesus.

RESOLUTION
To begin my daily time of prayer with still hands, empty hands, joined hands, and hands spread out for God to fill.

Generous Hands

If there is among you anyone in need, a member of your community in any of your towns . . . do not be hard-hearted or tight-fisted toward your needy neighbour. You should rather open your hand, willingly lending enough to meet the need, whatever it may be. (Deut. 15.7–8)

REFLECTION
'We make a living by what we get, but we make a life by what we give.' (Winston Churchill)

There are hands that help. There are hands that give. There are hands that assist others to the point of generosity. Sometimes we actually roll up our sleeves and get our hands dirty in helping other people. That is practical help. I am trying to deal with the waist-high grass at the back of our house. It looks an impossible assignment. Then along comes one of my sons and says, 'Dad, let me give you a hand.'

Again our hands are up for self-examination. What will they do today to lend a hand to other people? What did they do yesterday that was a practical help to others? Look at your hands as you think the question through. Take your time. Two days ago you made a list of your 'negatives'. Today is the chance to list your 'positives'.

The real question is, 'Are your hands openly generous or tight-fistedly stingy?' Compared with many people we are rich. So just how generous are your hands? Lent brings before us the three traditional themes of prayer, fasting and almsgiving. 'Almsgiving' may be a very old-fashioned word but the concept of sacrificial generosity which lies behind it is new in every age. Look at your hands. Are they recklessly generous when it comes to the needs of other people?

Some hands are busy making a living by what they can get. Other hands are equally busy making a life by what they give. Which hands are ours? Lent calls us to re-examine the priorities of our spending. Lent calls us to give to God's children in need. Again it is more than physical. Lent calls us to give sacrifically for the extension of the Kingdom of God on earth. How generous are you to other people? How sacrificial are you in your weekly commitment to the work of God through your parish church? Your hands will give you the answer.

PRAYER
Lord Christ, I spend so much energy hanging on to what I have. Help me to let go, just as you did when you left the Father's side to live as one of us. Loosen my grip on things and so free my heart to love and my hands to give; for your name's sake.

RESOLUTION
To give generously each week to a human need of my choosing; to give generously each week to at least one missionary society; to give each week a fixed proportion of my income to the life and ministry of my local church.

Greedy Hands

He [Jesus] fasted forty days and forty nights, and afterwards he was famished. The tempter came and said to him, 'If you are the Son of God, command these stones to become loaves of bread.' (Matt. 4.2–3)

REFLECTION

Greed is an excessive desire for food or wealth, although the concept can be applied to any need or appetite. In contrast, 'Fasting is the attitude of, "Lord, empty me of self." ' (H.H. Leavitt)

Lent is about fasting, a word which stands for the control of all our appetites. Need becomes greed when it is out of control.

Jesus knew what it was to be truly hungry. He had been in the desert without food for days. He saw the stones, picked them up, felt them. They looked like bread rolls, but what came to him was more than a desire to eat. He experienced something else. The idea formed in his mind. He would satisfy his own hunger and at the same time feed a hungry world.

He was alone with God, fasting and praying. He was preparing for the work God had given him to do which would end in the cross. The temptation to feed himself was an enticement to give way to human appetite, to put himself first. It was made the more attractive because of the associated idea of winning acceptance in the world by offering bread. All the time he knew that 'One does not live by bread alone, but by every word that comes from the mouth of God.'

Was he to carry out his ministry in his way or in God's way? In whose control was he? To whose will was he committed?

We look again at our hands. Who controls them? Are they merely at the dictate of our appetites or are they the servants of human will aligned with God's will?

Greed is need out of control. It is not that we need to deny the legitimacy of our needs. They are part of what it is to be human. Yet how easily the need of our hands becomes the greed of our hearts. Our hands can lead us deeper into our inner selves if we will let them.

Let me complete the saying of H.H. Leavitt, 'Fasting is the attitude of, "Lord, empty me of self." Prayer is the insistent cry of one's soul, "Lord, fill me with thyself." '

It is in fasting that we can distinguish the better between need and greed.

PRAYER
Lord, you have made me with all my needs, and what you have made is good. Teach me to discern between need and greed, that in everything I may be the instrument of your will carried out in your way.

RESOLUTION
To make an act of self-denial this Lent; to set aside each week a period of fasting.

FOR GROUP DISCUSSION *OR* INDIVIDUAL REFLECTION

1. How can we use this Lent to rediscover the meaning and joy of our Christian experience?
2. What place do you think silence or stillness should play before worship, during worship, after worship?
3. How generous should we be in our weekly giving to the Church? How generous should our parish be in giving to needs outside itself?
4. What is the value of fasting? How is it different from dieting? What role should fasting play in our lives as individuals or as a congregation?

Receiving Hands

Jesus said to them: 'I am the bread of life. Whoever comes to me will never be hungry, and whoever believes in me will never be thirsty.' (John 6.35)

REFLECTION

In the Lord's Prayer we pray, 'Give us today our daily bread.' Each day God responds, putting great blessings into our hands.

Perhaps this reflection would be better carried out at the end of the day, when we are able to look back and recall the good things which have come into our hands since we woke up this morning. Think back, then, over the past twenty-four hours and look at your hands. What good things did they receive? I suggest that you list your responses. Count your blessings.

We need God and we need each other. We depend upon God and we depend upon each other. We are taught that it is more blessed to give than to receive. (Acts 20.35) Only by being open to receive can other people share that blessing.

All our stories are different. In those stories most, if not all of us, can identify the good things we have received. So often we reach out our hands and they are filled. Once, when the family was younger, we were desperately short of money; a generous gift was placed in our hands. I have felt frightened and alone and someone has placed a comforting hand in mine. I recall another occasion when a point of misunderstanding was cleared up; the other person proffered a hand in reconciliation and acceptance.

There are graces also, spiritual blessings, given to us. Week by week we stretch out our hands and they are filled with the Bread of Life and the Cup of Everlasting Salvation.

Jesus loved little children. They were brought to him to have him place his hands on them and pray for them. Despite the disciples turning the children away, they in simple trust waited for the touch of the hands of Jesus who welcomed them.

Reflecting on the children gives me a new appreciation of our Lord's words, 'Unless you change and become like children, you will never enter the kingdom of heaven.' (Matt. 18.3) Like those children, I come to Jesus in simple and joyful trust. I know that he will not turn me away. I know that I belong. I know that I am his. In Communion I come to Jesus and I am received as I feed on him in my heart by faith.

PRAYER
For all the good things which my hands receive, I offer you my thanks, dear Lord. Give to me the expectant hands of a child, open to receive the good gifts of life. Above all, give me the heart of a child, open to receive you and your love; for love's sake.

RESOLUTION
To come to Jesus, ready to receive what he has for me this day.

Destructive Hands

*At the upper entrance they hacked the wooden trellis
with axes. And then, with hatchets and hammers, they
smashed all its carved work. They set your sanctuary
on fire; they desecrated the dwelling place of your
name bringing it to the ground.* (Ps. 74.5–7)

REFLECTION
Michelangelo's *Pieta* must be one of the greatest pieces
of sculpture in the world. I simply do not know how
hard, cold stone can be used to portray the deep emo-
tion and poignancy of the Mother holding the body of
her dead Son. But Michelangelo did it. These days,
however, you have to look at it in St Peter's Basilica,
Rome, through a protective screen of glass, since someone took a hammer to it.

Sometimes destruction has a religious motivation.
You may have seen the headless stone statues at Wells
Cathedral. The Puritans, in religious fervour, destroyed
them. Beautiful wooden carvings and sacred shrines
were hacked down, and sacred sanctuaries were used to
shelter horses.

You do not have to go far to view the work of destructive hands. Graffiti abounds; telephone boxes are regu-
larly 'trashed'; seats are slashed in public transport. All
are the work of destructive hands.

I have never been able to understand the attraction of
boxing, where the aim is to pummel the other person
into insensibility. There is the violence which our
hands perform and which, on television, forms a big
part of entertainment.

Violence we now learn is increasingly a feature of family life. There are concerns that we are spawning a violent society.

It is strange how personally, nationally and internationally we still act as though violence can itself create peace. Tolstoy warned, 'A good portion of the evils that afflict humanity is due to the erroneous belief that life can be made secure by violence.'

So we should look at our hands very carefully. Are they destructive hands? When are they raised to destroy, to punish, to hurt?

PRAYER
Lord, save me from the heat of temper and the fervour of the religious crusader which issues in hurt and harm; take from my heart the spirit of violence, and make my hands instruments of your peace; for Christ's sake.

RESOLUTION
Daily to seek the grace of God for the control of the impulses behind my hands.

Creative Hands

Let the favour of the Lord our God be upon us, and prosper for us the work of our hands — O prosper the work of our hands! (Ps. 90.17)

REFLECTION

In my left hand I held a beautiful piece of porcelain. It may have been hand painted. In my right hand I gripped a hammer. The congregation watched aghast as I struck the cup and as the shattered pieces fell to the ground. (The cup was a cracked one!) 'So hard to make, so easy to break', I said.

Beautiful things are generated by a creative mind, skilful hands and a big dose of patience and perseverance.

Human beings are made in the image of the Creator. We share his creativity. One person can take a list of words and write a poem. Another can start with an assembly of notes and finish with a symphony. Still others seem to have 'green fingers' and produce resplendent gardens. For yet others it is tapestry or cooking or knitting or playing the piano or painting.

Creative hands are hands in tune with a creative mind. What can your hands do? To answer this question, sit still and look at your hands. Making a list may be helpful. Do not overlook the seemingly ordinary: sewing on a button, fixing a leaking tap, giving the car an oilchange, offering hospitality, cooking a dinner. These things are just as important, just as creative as conducting an orchestra, performing intricate brain surgery or carrying off a national art prize.

When I use my hands creatively I am imaging the Creator in whose likeness I am made.

PRAYER
Creator God, help me to think your thoughts and to do your deeds. Take my hands and work through them. May what I do, whether it be humble or great in the world's eyes, be worthy of you whose Son worked at a carpenter's bench, even Jesus Christ our Lord.

RESOLUTION
To seek joy and satisfaction in all that I do, making it a creative offering to God.

Serving Hands

Then Jesus poured water into a basin and began to wash the disciples' feet and to wipe them with the towel that was tied around him. (John 13.5)

REFLECTION

> And after supper he washed their feet,
> for service, too, is sacrament.
> (F. Pratt Green)

What Jesus did with his hands tells us something profound about his inner nature. Service is sacrament, an outward sign of the inner reality.

When Jesus stooped down with basin and towel and washed the feet of his followers, he was giving them an important message. The service of others, humble, foot-washing service, is the essential character of true ministry. The world fusses about titles, order of precedence, protocol, status. The proper measure of greatness is to be found in this simple scene of basin and towel.

Again we examine our hands. Are they serving hands? A list of the services rendered to others by our hands is suggested, not to make us feel good, but to help us see the truth about ourselves. The result will be great thankfulness for God's grace in our lives, or the recognition that our hands do not yet bear much resemblance to Christ's.

There is another, deeper, message in the footwashing. Jesus was not just putting on an act. He was not merely seizing on a situation to teach them all a lesson. He was acting in conformity with his own inner nature. The foot-washing is a window into the character of Jesus. Jesus is like that in his very nature. God is like that. The God whom we worship, to whom we pray, whom we proclaim, is like that.

Christ's hands reveal his heart. Simple, practical, humble service is the outworking of his character of love. What story do our hands tell about our inner nature? What are we really like? St Paul says: 'In humility regard others as better than yourselves. Let each of you look not to your own interests, but to the interests of others. Let the same mind be in you that was in Christ Jesus . . .' (Phil. 2:3–5) Have we the mind of Christ?

PRAYER
Lord of the towel and basin, come and transform me by your love which washes and renews, so that I may be remade in the likeness of him whose very character is humble service, even Jesus the Saviour.

RESOLUTION
To discover today's unused but waiting basin and towel and to use them.

No Hands

Again Jesus entered the synagogue, and a man was there who had a withered hand. (Mark 3.1)

REFLECTION

As children riding bicycles we used to call out, 'Look, Mum, no hands.' It was an intrepid feat! It must be altogether different to have no hands at all. That happened for some of the thalidomide babies. There are those, like the Anglican priest whom I met in Capetown, whose hands were blown off when he opened a letter-bomb.

It is hard to imagine just how little I could have achieved today without my hands. Dressing, shaving, turning on a tap, cleaning my teeth — the simplest of things would no longer be possible. I could not even turn the pages of this book or find my place in the Bible. A list is called for once again. Write down the things which you have done or will do with your hands today. Do not miss the obvious: opening a door, ironing a shirt, writing a letter, feeding yourself.

Every day my hands are at my service. I take them for granted. In fact they are a great gift, wonderfully and intricately designed.

Look again at your hands. Move your fingers about. The movement of the joints is a superb piece of design. The capacity to join finger and thumb is the key to so much that we are able to do.

Our hands give us a sense of feeling. The feel of things is important — the smoothness of silk, the warmth of wool, the comfort of a favourite toy, the fur of the cat.

Some do not have this gift. Some can only remember. For my hands I give thanks.

PRAYER
Father, for the gift of my hands I thank you. Grant me grace to use my hands creatively, generously, usefully. Help me to be caring and sensitive towards those whose use of their hands is impaired; for Christ's sake.

RESOLUTION
To use my hands today and every day to do consciously and lovingly one creative thing.

Touched by God

The Spirit of the Lord God is upon me, because the Lord has anointed me. (Isa. 61.1)

REFLECTION

'Mum', one of my brothers called out, 'Mum, she touched me.' He was only little, one of my three brothers. It was his first close encounter with a girl. I cannot remember whether he was pleased or not, but she had touched him.

Our lives have been touched by God just as surely as a hand stretched out to touch us. Spend a few moments today remembering those times when you knew that you had been touched by God.

Although I have no memory of it, I am quite sure that at my baptism it was God who touched me, putting his mark on me, claiming me as his own. For me the hands of the bishop at confirmation conveyed that same sense of encounter. I could add the laying on of hands in ordination. Especially vivid is the touch of God in consecration as a bishop. There are for many of us other moments when the divine reality has been revealed to us with special clarity — times of answered prayer, of illumination, of reassurance. It may have been in a church service, in private prayer. It may have been in the quietness of a forest or standing on a mountain peak; it may have been as you looked in wonder at your newborn child. It may have been when you least expected it.

We tend, like the newspapers, to dwell on difficulties and disasters. We need to revisit the oases of our spiritual journey, the special moments of encouragement and reassurance, the times of illumination and encouragement. Revisit those oases and drink deeply at them. Know that God has touched you. His mark is on you. You are his.

PRAYER
Dear God, I often act as though you were far away. In reality you are always close to me. Help me to be more aware of your presence, more receptive to your touch. Anoint me now with the touch of your loving, renewing Spirit.

RESOLUTION
To stay in touch through prayer, through sacrament, through Scripture, through worship — to revisit the oases of my spiritual journey and to drink deeply at them.

Christ's Hands

People were bringing little children to Jesus in order that he might touch them. (Mark 10.13)

REFLECTION

I can still feel the touch of my mother's hands. There was love, comfort, cooling in her touch, when as a child I was sick or awoke in terror in the middle of a nightmare.

Jewish mothers wanted their children to be blessed by important and distinguished rabbis. Perhaps this is the background to the story pictured here as the mothers brought their children to Jesus that he might touch them. It is a beautiful scene, sometimes over-sentimentalized. Yet the touch of Jesus conveys acceptance, welcome, inclusion, love, care, self-worth. It is a blessing felt as much by the mothers as by the children.

Jesus did great things with his hands. The touch of the hands of Jesus must indeed have been something special. His touch brought peace and joy to troubled hearts. His touch gave healing to the sick, sight to the blind, speech to the mute, hearing to the deaf, release to the paralysed. His touch even raised the dead. Day by day his hands gave grace and blessing.

His hands still do all of those things. They are the hands which for love's sake were nailed to the cross. 'See from his head, his hands, his feet, sorrow and love flow mingled down.' Those hands were stilled by death. Now they are resurrection hands. Christ showed them to Thomas in his doubt and disbelief. 'Thomas, reach out your hands and touch and examine.' Those hands brought forth the affirmation of faith, 'My Lord and my God'.

Look at the hands of Christ. Seek the healing and blessing and acceptance of his touch.

PRAYER
Lord Jesus Christ, show me your hands that I may be strengthened in my faith; touch me with your hands that I may receive that peace and wholeness which are your gifts; enfold me in your embrace that I may know that I am yours, wholly and forever.

RESOLUTION
To be Christ's hands in my encounter with someone today — the channel of his love, peace, hope and healing.

FOR GROUP DISCUSSION OR INDIVIDUAL REFLECTION

1. What can children teach us about how to receive naturally and joyfully from God and others?

2. In what ways is your congregation seen by outsiders as a serving community, reflecting the foot-washing Christ? How can your church respond better to the needs of your community?

3. You turn to exchange the greeting of peace with the person next to you in the pew. Suddenly you discover that the person has no hands. How would you feel? What would you do or say? What will your body language tell the other person?

4. What is the significance of 'touch' in the ministry of the Church? You might consider the place of 'touch' in baptism, confirmation, the greeting of peace in the service and the laying on of hands in the healing ministry. Do not feel restricted to these suggestions.

Our Feet

SUNDAY (LENT 2) · DAY 12

Down to Earth

Christ Jesus emptied himself, taking the form of a slave, being born in human likeness. (Phil. 2.7)

REFLECTION

Our feet — that is where the leather hits the road! Each week in Lent we will be taking a different part of the human body and seeing its significance for us as God's people.

So, put your feet together on the floor and look at them. They may be old feet or young; they may be comfortable or corned, bouncy or bunioned. But they are your feet. They are the point of contact between you and God's created world.

Down the Christian centuries there have been those who have regarded the created world as evil. Only the things of the spirit are good, they said. It was not that they merely practised simplicity, even asceticism. They went further. They renounced the world. But, no matter how high your head is in the clouds, your feet bring you down to earth. This is God's world. It is upon his earth that we walk, amidst the things of his creation.

This brings us to a key Christian teaching. It is called the incarnation. The Jesus who walked this earth was both God and human. He emptied himself of his rightful glory and took human form.

Because of the incarnation we can never be totally world-renouncing. The earth that we walk is God's, spoiled by us sometimes, but still bearing the stamp of the Creator. God in Christ became part of this world, subject to it. He, the truly spiritual being, walked this earth on feet like ours.

Our immediate vocation, then, is to live as part of this order. We are to follow in the footsteps of Jesus. That means that we do not regard other people with a spiritual superiority. We walk alongside them, just as he did.

Our feet, and let us look at them again, anchor us in time and space. This is a reminder of the immediacy and relevance of the gospel. The good news is for here and now on this earth, wearing these shoes. It is important for us as Christians to make sure that our feet touch the ground. Part of us soars to heights unknown. Our feet keep us in touch with this world.

PRAYER

Lord Jesus, we thank you for our feet and for the earth upon which they tread. Keep us in touch with the reality of life and help us to walk worthy of our vocation as co-workers and co-walkers with you.

RESOLUTION

To come alongside others and walk with them as a companion; to seek that understanding which comes from walking in other people's shoes.

Tethered Feet

The tribune came, arrested Paul, and ordered him to be bound with two chains. (Acts 21.33)

REFLECTION

Perhaps you know the parody of the well-known hymn:

> Like a mighty army
> moves the Church of God;
> We're forever treading
> where we've always trod.

Dogs are chained up. Birds have their wings clipped. Noble jungle cats pace up and down at the bars of their cages. Paul's missionary travels are brought to an end by confinement.

The Christian Church often finds itself bound by convention, tradition and fear, treading the well-worn familiar tracks instead of the exciting venture of new paths. Five years serving on a parish church council can be more like one year repeated five times over!

The same can happen in our own personal lives for Christ. Sometimes it is as though we were tethered to a post by a rope so that we can only travel in a circle.

So I am looking at my feet again. I suggest you look at yours. Are they bound or are they free? Do they stick to the tried and true track, the well-worn way of custom and convention; or are they free to strike out on new adventures of faith?

Our feet can be visible pointers to our spirits. God is not static, but dynamic. He calls us to walk new paths, think new thoughts, undertake new tasks, take new risks. Have we discovered and explored the glorious liberty of the children of God?

We need to look at our feet, examine them closely and ask fearlessly — where are these feet of mine taking me? Is the goal worthwhile?

PRAYER
Lord God, free me from all that shackles, limits and oppresses me; give me feet ready to do your bidding; above all help me to discover in my life the glorious liberty of being your child.

RESOLUTION
To begin to leave behind today all that limits and binds me and to live as one who has been freed by Christ.

Have Feet, Will Travel

*A Samaritan while travelling came near him; and
when he saw him, he was moved with pity. He went to
him . . .* (Luke 10.33–4)

REFLECTION
'I shall pass through this world but once. Any good
thing therefore that I can do, or any kindness that I can
show to any human being, let me do it now. Let me not
defer it or neglect it, for I shall not pass this way again.'
(Stephen Grellet)

That was not the impulse which controlled the feet
of those two religious office bearers who came upon the
beaten-up traveller by the roadside. They had religious
duties to perform. Their feet helped to speed them
away from the disagreeable sight which, except for
their strength of mind, might have become a real
interruption.

I condemn them. But when have my feet done a simi-
lar thing? When have my feet conveyed me quickly
from the scene of need? When have they helped me to
avoid the weekly button sellers on the street corners
representing a thousand and one good causes and en-
abled me to walk by on the other side?

Then came the despised foreigner whose religion
lacked credentials, whose place in society was beneath
notice and who belonged to a third-rate race. It is this
traveller who stops, is deeply moved, and whose feet
bring him to the side of the bruised and battered victim.

Today, this very day, it is you and I who are the
travellers. We have made our plans for the day. We

know where we are going and it is in the diary. The course is set. Look out for today's interruption. Will we see it as an opportunity? Someone's need will cross our path unexpectedly today. It may come to us through a telephone call or in a letter. It will mean changing our plans, adjusting our priorities, going out of our way. How will our feet respond?

There are those whose feet help them to pass by on the other side. There are those whose feet enable them to go to others in their need. Just what kind of feet are ours?

One thing is certain, 'I shall not pass this way again.'

PRAYER
Loving Lord, as you soften my heart with compassion for others in their need, so turn my feet towards them. May my heart become yours, my feet your feet.

RESOLUTION
To seize today's unexpected opportunity for loving service and to do it joyfully.

Blistered Feet

Then Jesus poured water into a basin and began to wash the disciples' feet and to wipe them with the towel that was tied around him. (John 13.5)

REFLECTION

I watched as the boys and girls from the school came in from their fund-raising walkathon. Some were just hobbling, their feet obviously blistered. I think everyone was glad to have a hot shower; some needed to soak their feet in warm water; a few needed special treatment.

It is tough journeying for Christ. The hymn makes it sound glamorous, 'O let me see thy footmarks, And in them plant mine own.' In reality commitment to Christ is costly. It is hard work. It means giving time and energy and money. It means carrying a cross. It means blisters on your feet.

Perhaps your feet have felt that way as you have sought to be faithful to our Lord. The load seems to fall so often upon the faithful few. It is then that Christ takes the basin and towel and washes our feet. Our God is a God who empties himself of glory to be one of us. Our God is one who gets alongside and identifies with the weak and helpless and oppressed, the alienated and abandoned, the weary and worn. Our God is one who washes feet.

One writer, I have forgotten who, applies the foot-washing to the moment of reception by God after death. Some might stress judgement. This writer points to gentle foot-washing. After our death we will be met by Jesus and he will have the basin and towel. He will be ready to wash away the pains and stresses and tiredness, making us ready for the Kingdom. He will say, 'Phillip, it has been tough, I know. Let me wash your feet.'

Today we bring our tired and blistered feet — our tired and blistered selves — to Christ for the comfort and balm and healing of his washing.

PRAYER
Lord, I come to you weary, even disheartened, for the journey is long and the task so difficult. Come and wash not only my feet, but my hands and my head also, that I may be refreshed and renewed in my whole being; I ask it in Christ's name.

RESOLUTION
To let Christ minister to me, calming and refreshing and renewing me.

No Feet

In Lystra there was a man sitting who could not use his feet and had never walked, for he had been crippled from birth. (Acts 14.8)

REFLECTION

'I used to complain that I had no shoes, until I met someone who had no feet.'

There are those who have no feet because of an accident or disease or because they were born that way. There are those whose feet have ceased to function properly.

Today let those of us who have feet which still serve us look at them with wonder and thanksgiving. Our feet serve us day by day. We notice them when we get a corn, but generally our feet are taken for granted. I can: walk, run, jump, kick a ball, drive a car, ride a bicycle, walk in the garden, swim in the sea, climb a mountain, make my selection of goods in the supermarket, stand to sing God's praises. This is all possible because I have feet.

Some are even able to paint pictures holding the brush with their feet.

Let us give thanks for our feet.

But what about those who have no feet? The community is not good at accepting people who have an obvious physical disability. Is the Church any better? We tend to shy away from people who have a physical disability. Our body language soon tells them that we are not comfortable. Yet they are fully human beings who need not pity but acceptance. They need the dignity of being treated as truly and fully human. They are not disabled persons, they are persons who have a disability!

There is another question. How do those who cannot walk at all, or who have difficulty in walking, get on in our churches? Are there handrails? Is there wheelchair access? Are the doors and aisles wide enough? Is there a ready, sensitive hand if needed, but respect also for those who wish to manage for themselves?

In one way or another every single one of us needs the acceptance and the healing of Christ. There is a real ministry in ensuring equality of access.

PRAYER
Lord, I thank you for my feet and for all the things which they enable me to do. Deliver us from any attitude or neglect which puts a barrier between you and those who need your love.

RESOLUTION
To give thanks for all the things which my feet enable me to do.

FRIDAY · DAY 17

Beautiful Feet

How beautiful upon the mountains are the feet of the messenger who announces peace, who brings good news, who announces salvation . . . (Isa. 52.7)

REFLECTION

We hear of beautiful eyes, beautiful hands, beautiful faces, even a beautiful nose, but rarely do we speak of beautiful feet.

Perhaps that is because we think of our feet primarily as a means of transport. The feet of those who serve God as his messengers are described as beautiful. Beautiful are the feet of God's messengers who usher in peace where the world knows only conflict and discord. Beautiful are the feet which bring good news to a society whose daily diet so often consists of disaster and disappointment, failure and frustration, recession and depression. Beautiful are the feet which carry the announcement of God's purpose of salvation, which proclaim that the Lord reigns. How much of our feet time and feet energy do we put into being beautiful feet? We spend a deal of time, even expense making sure about our face and hair. What about our feet?

Our feet take us to those who know nothing of God's love in Jesus Christ. In fact Jesus tells us to leave the ninety-nine and let our feet take us to the one who is lost. In this Decade of Evangelism we are discovering all over again what that means.

Our religious feet take us to worship and Bible study and prayer group and the like, but they seem to have lost their way when it comes to entering the community of non-believers.

All around us are people who need peace, good news and salvation. They will only experience these things when we use our feet to take us to them, to move amongst them, to be alongside them.

At the end of the Holy Communion service each Sunday the deacon dismisses us saying, 'Go in peace to love and serve the Lord.' The truth is that the real work for God only begins when our feet take us outside.

PRAYER
Lord, I want to be your feet, bearing your love and light to the world; as I come alongside those who do not know you, may my feet grow beautiful as the messengers of your peace and good news and salvation.

RESOLUTION
To ensure that the very feet which take me amongst fellow Christians also carry me to those who do not share my faith.

Christ's Feet

While they were talking and discussing, Jesus himself came near and went with them. (Luke 24.15)

REFLECTION

> See from his head, his hands, his feet,
> sorrow and love flow mingled down.
> *(Isaac Watts)*

Today we spend some time looking at the feet of our Saviour — the feet which were washed by the tears and dried with the hair of one sinful woman — those feet which carried him up the hill of Calvary — those feet which, according to tradition, were nailed to the cross — those feet which carried the Risen Lord out of the tomb into the new light of resurrection life.

Especially let us attend to the resurrection feet of Jesus. Two of his followers were walking to Emmaus, discussing the tragic events of the past few days. Their hearts were heavy, their hopes shattered. Without their realizing it, a wonderful thing occurred. The Risen Jesus came near and walked alongside them. They did not recognize him at first, but they took the opportunity to empty out the whole sad story to this unexpected companion who seemed so sympathetic. Only later, when he took the bread and blessed and broke it, did they tumble to the truth. Jesus was alive. He was with them. He was their companion.

We all journey on in our lives. Sometimes the sun is shining and our step is light and springy. We are at peace and all seems well. Then there are those days when all seems dark and pointless. Life mocks us; love gets knocked down whilst evil flourishes. Dark days come to us all. Where is Christ at such times? He is beside you. His feet have brought him to you once again. He is listening. He cares. You may not even recognize him. You may not identify him. Like those early followers you may be slow to discern. But here is the wonderful truth of the resurrection. It means that Christ is risen. Already he is fulfilling his promise to be with us until the end of time.

'Jesus himself came near and went with them.' He walks with you. He is your fellow traveller. Listen to the welcome sound of his feet.

PRAYER
Risen Lord, help me to walk each day in the faith that you walk with me. Even through the valley of the darkest shadow, you are with me. Stay close to me as my constant companion, I pray you.

RESOLUTION
To walk each day as in the presence of Christ; to set aside a time each day to speak to my companion on the way.

FOR GROUP DISCUSSION *OR* INDIVIDUAL REFLECTION

1. What does it mean to live in the world but not of the world? How is this evident in the life of Christ? How is it evident in the life of your congregation?

2. In what ways is the work of the Church today being limited and bound by convention or fear or some other force? In what ways does the Church need to break out and travel new paths?

3. Our Lord says, 'Come to me all who labour and are heavy-laden, and I will give you rest.' Does the life of your parish make this invitation a reality for people?

4. How does your parish provide for people with disabilities? What message does a lack of facilities give to people with disabilities? How can your parish do better?

Our Eyes

SUNDAY (LENT 3) · DAY 19

Eyes of Faith

Have you believed because you have seen me? Blessed are those who have not seen and yet have come to believe. (John 20.29)

REFLECTION

Jesus, these eyes have never seen
that radiant form of thine;
the veil of sense hangs dark between
thy blessed face and mine.

I see thee not, I hear thee not,
yet thou art oft with me;
and earth hath ne'er so dear a spot
as where I meet with thee.

(*R. Palmer*)

This week it is our eyes that are up for contemplation. So perhaps a mirror is needed, for most of us depend upon our eyes and few of us are acquainted with them. I remember my mother saying to one of my brothers,

'Look at your dirty face.' He answered, 'I can't. I'm behind it!' It is the same with our eyes.

Jesus points us to the eyes of faith and gives a special blessing to those 'who have not seen and yet have come to believe'. That blessing is for you and for me. We did not see him in Mary's arms. We were not there when he taught in the synagogue, healed the sick, raised the dead. We caught no sight of him on the infamous day of his crucifixion. We were not amongst those who saw him wonderfully risen from the dead and who believed on the basis of their eyes.

We have the evidence of Scripture. We have the inspiring example of the great ones, like Peter, who were so convinced of Christ's defeat of death that they would rather die than deny their faith in their Lord risen from the dead. We have also read of the faith of the saints in every age; those, like us, who have not seen and yet have believed. But belief or faith is a step which we must each take for ourselves, a discovery which each of us has to make individually through the eyes of faith.

It is as though I were crossing a deep and dangerous torrent, unable to see the sure footholds just below the surface. Others tell me they are there but I cannot see them. I can turn back. Or I can take the first step and discover the truth for myself. That is why some people talk about the leap of faith. The confirmation comes only as I take that crucial first step.

'Faith is the assurance of things hoped for, the conviction of things not seen.' (Heb. 11.1)

PRAYER
O Lord, increase our faith, strengthen us and confirm us in thy true faith; endue us with wisdom, charity, chastity and patience, in all our adversities. Sweet

Jesus, say amen. (From a seventeenth-century anthem).

RESOLUTION
To trust in the presence and power of God even on the darkest days.

Open Eyes

Consider the lilies of the field, how they grow; they neither toil nor spin, yet I tell you, even Solomon in all his glory was not clothed like one of these. (Matt. 6.28–9)

REFLECTION

> I used to like to hear him admire the beauty of a flower; it was a kind of gratitude to the flower itself, and a personal love for its delicate form and colour. I seem to remember him gently touching a flower he delighted in; it was the simple admiration that a child might have. (Francis Darwin, speaking of his father, Charles Darwin)

I shall never forget the day I first wore spectacles. I stepped outside my room at theological college wearing my glasses for the first time. In the distance were trees, turning green with the return of spring. It was an amazing sight. I could see more than a hazy colour. I could actually see the leaves, their shape and form and individuality.

I think it must have been vanity which delayed my having my eyes tested. Well, for the next few days, it was as though I were seeing everything for the first time, especially things in the distance, for I was short-sighted.

We can all be short-sighted at times. What beauty will you see about you today? The media is preoccupied with disaster. Modern cities abound in ugliness. The loveliness of nature has suffered wholesale devastation. Yet there is beauty all around us, if we have eyes to see.

It is through the gateway of the eye that we can take in the beauty of God's created world. I think of beautiful faces — the fresh faces of happy, bright-eyed children; the wrinkled faces of older, serene, wise ones, in the eventide of life, aged, but with their own brand of beauty. I think of the breathtaking beauty of the Grand Canyon, the serenity and majesty of the Tasmanian forests, the beauty of Coventry Cathedral, the verdant valley below as you come over the Sidling towards Scottsdale. The list is endless. All such beauty needs the eye to comprehend it. Eyesight is a great gift from God. It is capable of receiving beautiful messages.

'Behold the lilies of the field . . .'

PRAYER
Lord, help me to focus on all that is beautiful around me; then to see beyond the outward and visible to your beauty as Source and Creator of all.

RESOLUTION
To see as though for the first time the beauty that is all around me and to thank God for it.

Closed Eyes

*I will both lie down and sleep in peace; for you alone,
O Lord, make me lie down in safety.* (Psalm 4.8)

REFLECTION

Sancho Panza, the servant of Don Quixote, said, 'Blessings on him who first invented sleep. It covers a man all over, thoughts and all, like a cloak.'

It is good that our eyes are fitted with lids. For sleep, as the Psalmist reminds us, is a priceless gift of God. (Ps. 127.2)

The truth is that we are not made to stay awake all the time. We are not meant to work ceaselessly. 'The night comes when no one may work.' A lot happens while we close our eyes in sleep. Physically we are restored, refreshed, renewed. In other words, we rest but our creating, caring God is at work for our good.

In sleep we are also compelled to let go of the control of things. Some of us are accustomed to having the reins of life firmly in our hands, or so we think. Sleep reminds us that we are not the ones who rule things. God is the one who reigns. When we are least able to care for ourselves, then we entrust ourselves into his care.

When our eyes close in sleep God is at work in other ways too. I can think of the times when I have received a letter which demands a response. I simply cannot see how to reply. The waste-paper basket fills with discarded attempts. In the end I am compelled to leave it. It often happens that next morning when I awake I have an idea. Some might say that the brain continues to work while we are asleep. That may be true. Still I want to leave room for God.

There are those who cannot sleep. There may be no quick and easy solution for sleeplessness. Part of it is putting ourselves consciously into the hands of God in faith and trust. It means laying aside each night the strivings of the day's work, knowing that 'it is in vain that you rise early and go so late to rest'.

We can learn something from Christ here. Even as he closed his eyes in death, Jesus placed himself confidently in God's hands. 'Father, into your hands I commit my spirit.'

'I will both lie down and sleep in peace; for you alone, O Lord, make me lie down in safety.'

PRAYER
Lord God, you are the one who neither slumbers nor sleeps; save me from assuming your role; give me tonight and every night the recreating gift of undisturbed sleep.

RESOLUTION
Consciously, each night to commit myself to the care of God, ready to accept the gift of sleep.

Tears

Jesus began to weep. (John 11.35)

REFLECTION

Like us, Jesus wept. 'Tears are God's gift sent to help wash away our sorrows.' Those moving words are by Paul Arnott, a young priest in my diocese. He and Rosanne have recorded their experience of the death of an infant son due to sudden infant death syndrome in a beautiful book entitled *No Time to Say Goodbye*.

Our eyes are not only for seeing. They are also the scene of our tears. Tears are all right.

Jesus was a 'man of sorrows and acquainted with grief'. He wept over Jerusalem. He wept at Bethany. Was his weeping for the death of Lazarus or was it at the lack of faith displayed? Perhaps it was for both. 'Jesus wept.' That must be the shortest but must poignant sentence in the whole of the Bible.

Yes, it is all right for us to cry. Indeed it is important to do our grieving well, whether it be for the loss of a person or a pet or a position. If we do not express our grief it will come out later in destructive ways, bitter feelings, bitter words, unhealed hurts. We have all met people who have shrivelled up inside because of an ungrieved-for loss.

Perhaps that is part of the meaning behind the beatitude, 'Blessed are those who mourn, for they shall be comforted.' (Matt. 5.4) If we can learn to mourn, to grieve, to express that grief, to cry, then comfort will come, healing will begin. It is all right for men to cry as well as women. 'Real men don't cry', is the macho message of the Australian male stereotype. It betrays a false understanding of humanity and a total ignorance of grief as a necessary first step on the path of healing.

As well as our tears there are the tears of other people. There is a real ministry towards those who grieve. We have to learn to 'weep with those who weep'. Years ago I was called out in the early hours of the morning to the home of a parishioner whose husband had died in hospital. She talked; I listened. We stared into the fire. She wept and I wept with her. It was a start. This is a ministry which needs few words. The prerequisite is a heart which is open to bear and share the tears of sorrow.

PRAYER
O Lord, draw near to me in my losses and griefs and weep with me. But more, help me to come close to others in their sadness that I may weep with them. May we accept our tears as your gift sent to help wash away our sorrows.

RESOLUTION
To grieve well; and to weep with those who weep.

No Eyes

The blind man said to him [Jesus] 'My teacher, let me see again.' (Mark 10.51)

REFLECTION
Nothing clears the mind so much as the knowledge that tomorrow you are to die! Perhaps we only realize the true value of things when their loss is threatened.

The value of eyesight is sharpened by trying to imagine what it would be like if we could not see. At Richmond in Tasmania there is a solitary cell, part of the old convict gaol. Tourists may enter it and close the door and experience a little of what it was like to be placed in solitary confinement. Even then it is not real. You know that the door will open to admit the light and that you will be allowed out into the world again. The loneliness, the isolation — these things are harder to imagine. Experiences like that, day after day, sent some prisoners mad.

Our eyes, then, are more than intricate and complex receivers of images. They provide a vital contact with the world around. Eyes, for most of us, are a significant link with that world. Take the eyes away and we lose a great deal in terms of relationships. I look at people and distinguish one from another. There is the face and form of a friend. Here is the face and form of someone I love dearly. My eyes help me to distinguish, to recognize, to relate. To have no eyesight is to face forces of isolation and separation which we do not often think about.

Even my memories depend upon my eyes. Memories are like a photograph album, reminders of people and places and occasions from the past. Memories are moving pictures, videos, reruns of so much that in the past I took in visually. I do not say that people without sight have no memory. For many of us at any rate, there is a large visual component to the capacity to recall as well as to the content of that recollection.

My eyesight has a place in worship. I can read the prayers; I can see the candles on the holy table radiating their message about the light of the world. I can see the sacrament in my hand. I can see the words of the hymn. I can see the one who is exchanging the greeting of peace with me.

Just how welcome is the person who has little or no sight? What provision is made for them in worship? Or do we isolate them even more by our failure to provide for persons with disabilities?

Sometimes it is we who are blind — blind to the real needs of people. Sometimes it is the Church which is blind — blind to its opportunities and obligations.

PRAYER
Lord God, forgive the blindness which prevents our responding to the needs of your people; open our eyes, that seeing we may be ready to meet the rightful claims of others upon us.

RESOLUTION
To become more aware of the blind spots in my own life and in the life of the local church.

Attentive Eyes

My eyes have seen your salvation, which you have prepared in the presence of all peoples. (Luke 2.30–1)

REFLECTION

The basic rule in all ball games is, 'Keep your eye on the ball.' This applies whether you are kicking or hitting or fielding a ball. Success requires concentrating exclusively on the ball.

It is the same in other spheres. Hitting the bull's-eye depends upon careful sighting. Passing the baton in the relay demands deliberately focused attention by both giver and receiver.

What then is the focus of our lives? To what do we give our attention? What is our aim or goal? To what do our eyes actually attend?

Fix on the wrong thing and it will let you down. For example, it is possible for the focus of faith to light upon a particular building or priest or preacher or prayer book. But buildings crumble, priests move on, preachers fade and liturgies change.

We live in a world of constantly changing language and customs and culture. Moreover, as Toffler warned us, these things are changing at an ever-increasing rate. I am not speaking merely of preferences. We all have those. I am speaking of the focus of our concentration. I am speaking of the danger of mistaking the signs and symbols of God's unchanging presence for the reality of that presence.

Our eyes must be fixed on Jesus Christ, for he alone is the same yesterday, today, and forever. For the rest, 'time like an ever-rolling stream' bears all else away. Little wonder that H.F. Lyte, in his famous hymn, wrote, 'Change and decay in all around I see: O thou who changest not, abide with me.' It is to Jesus that we look, the author and finisher of our faith. To him we attend. He is the object of our attentive gaze.

PRAYER
O God, help me to change gracefully in an ever-changing world, but always to have you firmly in my gaze, for you alone are constant, abiding and faithful.

RESOLUTION
To loosen my grip on the things of lesser worth, so that I may be the more firmly attached to God in Christ.

The Eyes of Christ

The Lord turned and looked at Peter. Then Peter remembered the word of the Lord, how he had said to him, 'Before the cock crows today, you will deny me three times.' And he went out and wept bitterly. (Luke 22.61–2)

REFLECTION
I will never forget the look in the eyes of an old friend and parishioner who died some years ago. He was on a respirator and could not speak to me. He was desperately ill and, I think, knew that he would die shortly. I prayed and laid hands on him in blessing and commendation.

Still there was something undone, a concern he had, a message he wanted to give me. All he had were his eyes to convey that message. What was it? I made an informed guess. I could see that I was right. I promised him that I would fulfil his last wish.

Our eyes receive images. They also send out messages. One look can say a lot! The eye can send a withering look that turns people off. It is also capable of conveying love and understanding. What do people see in our eyes?

It is time for us in our meditations to look into the eyes of Jesus Christ. They are an open window into his heart. I imagine that those eyes must have twinkled with amusement as he verbally painted the ridiculous picture of someone trying to remove a log from their eyes. We know that his eyes filled with tears as he looked over the city of Jerusalem. He looked with love on the children brought to him for blessing. There was strength in his eyes when he commanded the storm to be still; and judgement when he rebuked the scribes and Pharisees.

It might help the Bible to come alive if we were to read it, trying to see in our imagination the eyes of Jesus, the way he looked at other people. For example, there was the terrible night when Peter denied Christ three times, just as Jesus had predicted. The Lord turned and looked at Peter. It was too much for the fisherman turned disciple. He went out and wept.

What did the eyes of Jesus convey? 'I told you so, you failure!' More likely it was a look of understanding love, which would have been the harder to take. It was a look which brought Peter to tears of repentance.

The eyes of Christ are upon us. Look at those eyes. What message do they convey to us?

PRAYER
Help me, O Lord, to see in your eyes a look of warning, judgement and rebuke; may I see also your look of understanding, love and forgiveness so that the application of these qualities to my life may issue in reformation and renewal.

RESOLUTION
To think and speak and act at all times as in the sight of Christ.

FOR GROUP DISCUSSION *OR*
INDIVIDUAL REFLECTION

1. What does the expression 'a leap of faith' mean to you? Tell others in the group how you came to be a person of faith in Jesus Christ. Discuss how others can be helped to come to that point.

2. What are the most beautiful sights that you have seen? Share together experiences of great beauty which remain vivid in the memory. What part do your eyes play in those memories?

3. What should be the local church's ministry with those whose sight is impaired? If you were such a person, what would you find of relevance in your local church's programme?

4. Someone says, 'Tears are a sign of weakness. If one must cry it is a personal matter. We should do our weeping in private.' Do you agree?

Our Tongues

SUNDAY (LENT 4) · DAY 26

Praising Tongue

*O come, let us sing to the Lord; let us make a joyful
noise to the rock of our salvation!* (Ps. 95.1)

REFLECTION
This week our thoughts will be centred on our tongues,
described in the letter of James as the smallest but most
dangerous part of the human body.

Even so, Charles Wesley wanted more than one!
'O for a thousand tongues to sing my dear redeemer's
praise.'

What words of praise for the goodness and greatness
of God are on my lips today? What song of praise
springs from my heart as I contemplate his love for me?
Praise is not merely something which we do. Praise is
evoked in us by God himself.

Partly, praise is a response to what God has done —
in creation, in salvation, in sanctification. Or we look
at the beauty of a sunset, the faces of children, the
wonder of the cross, the joy of the resurrection — and
praise flows from the heart through the tongue.

Partly, and perhaps more deeply, praise is a response to what God is in himself. He is the transcendent, unknowable one, yet the ever-present, imminent one whose grace goes before every movement of goodness and love within us. Praise then tips over into awe and wonder, a commodity seemingly in short supply in worship.

Praise may need no words at all. It is like two lovers content in one another's company, sitting, looking at one another, holding hands. Teased about his daily visits to the parish church and asked what it was he did when he went there, the simple villager replied, 'I just sits and looks at 'im, and 'e looks at me.' That wordless, silent contemplation of God is praise and adoration.

A little exercise is suggested. Sit quietly and contemplate the wonder and glory of the being and love of God. Write down some words of praise. You might choose prose; you might prefer verse, like a hymn.

Then offer your words to God as a song. Make up your own tune. No one else can hear it! Repeat it several times through the day, your own song of praise to the God who watches over you, walks with you and dwells within you. 'O come, let us sing to the Lord.'

PRAYER
Lord, I have only one tongue, but I offer it in praise of you. I love you; I want you; I need you; I praise you. You are my God and I adore you.

RESOLUTION
To put praise in my daily prayers — ahead of asking.

Destructive Tongue

How great a forest is set ablaze by a small fire! And the tongue is a fire. (Jas. 3.5–6)

REFLECTION
Do not be fooled by size. Goliath was, and paid with his life at the hands of the much smaller David. Our tongues are small. They are also capable of great destruction.

The best known biblical passage about the human tongue is in the third chapter of the letter of James. 'The tongue is a small member', he writes, 'yet it boasts of great exploits.' What exploits do our tongues boast of? James likens the tongue to the bit in the mouth of the horse. Control the mouth and you control the animal. The whole body is kept in check with bit and bridle.

We are forced to ask ourselves about the use of our tongues, about the control of our tongues, about the training of our tongues. Every day we speak to people individually and in groups. What we say can have an enormous effect, often stronger than we realize. Will we not some day answer on the basis of what we have said; be judged on the basis of what we have said?

There is a terrible warning in the words of James.

How great a forest is set ablaze by a small fire! And the tongue is a fire. The tongue is placed among our members as a world of iniquity; it stains the whole body, sets on fire the cycle of nature, and is itself set on fire by hell. For every species of beast and bird, of reptile and sea creature, can be tamed and has been tamed by the human species, but no one can tame the tongue — a restless evil, full of deadly poison. With it we bless the Lord and Father, and with it we curse those who are made in the likeness of God. (Jas. 3.5–9)

Do we ever speak in order to put others down? Do we speak with the intention of hurting? Are we gossips? Do we talk ceaselessly and needlessly?

Do we feel that God has given us the answers to other people's questions and needs and problems, so that we take upon ourselves the responsibility for telling them what to do? In the process we may well impose our own views upon other people, assert our power over them, deprive them of the dignity of being responsible for their own lives and actions.

I am not the first to note that God has given us one tongue but two ears, so that we might spend twice as much time in listening as we do in speaking.

PRAYER
Father, help me to deal with the bitterness in my heart before it can reach my tongue. If my speech cannot be gracious give me the gift of silence; if I must gossip let it be only of you and of your goodness.

RESOLUTION
If I cannot say it as to God, I will not say it at all.

Silent Tongue

For everything there is a season, and a time for every matter under heaven: . . . a time to keep silence, and a time to speak. (Eccles. 3.1, 7)

REFLECTION

There is no shortage of clever sayings about silence. They range from Miguel de Cervantes, 'A closed mouth catches no flies'; through Abraham Lincoln, 'Better to remain silent and be thought a fool than to speak and remove all doubt'; to Sydney Smith, 'He had occasional flashes of silence that made his conversation perfectly delightful.'

Today we think about the still tongue, about silence. There is the 'silence of eternity, interpreted by love', the silence of outer space, the silence of deep commitment, the silence of lovers, the silence of God.

Silence is a great and positive possession; it is more than the mere absence of sound. It is in itself a gift, a grace.

It is the silent tongue which is linked to the listening ear and the caring heart. We can be too quick to proffer advice and consolation, when what is needed is the capacity to be quiet and to listen. Other people need us to be silent that they may speak. They need to empty out. Our silence is a ministry.

There is also the silence of confidentiality. No real relationship of trust can exist without the assurance that our tongues do not vibrate with the things which we have taken in with our ears. Can we keep a confidence? When did we last betray a trust? We need to ask what part silence plays in our prayers. Do we listen to God before we speak? What part does silence play in the public worship of the Church? Do we use it?

Which would we rather have from God — the gift of wise speech or the gift of caring, listening silence?

There is an old sixteenth-century prayer which asks the Saviour to teach us the silence of humility, the silence of wisdom, the silence of love, the silence of perfection and the silence of faith. These things — humility, wisdom, love, perfection, faith — are some of the fruits of creative silence, that silence which is not emptiness but which is filled with the things of God and of his goodness.

We may discover that silence is golden in ways which we had never thought of before.

PRAYER
You have uttered one Word and that Word is your Son, whom you utter forever in everlasting silence. May my soul in silence hear it. (After John of the Cross.)

RESOLUTION
To make room for silence in my prayers, in my life, and in my heart; and to seek discernment as to when to speak and when to remain silent.

Gracious Tongue

Let your speech always be gracious, seasoned with salt, so that you may know how you ought to answer everyone. (Col. 4.6)

REFLECTION

Yesterday's sayings about silence need their counter-balance. It comes in the book of Ecclesiasticus, 'Never remain silent when a word might put things right.' (Ecclus. 4.23)

If it is right on occasions to be silent; it is also on other occasions wrong to remain silent. When have you remained silent when you ought to have spoken? Why did you not speak? What constrained you?

When we have hurt someone, failed them, disappointed them, what a difference it makes to say, 'I am sorry. It was my fault. Please forgive me.'

Someone gets the prize or the promotion or the recognition which we would have liked. What a difference it makes to say, 'Congratulations, I am really pleased for you.'

These are gracious words. They promote love and peace and harmony; they raise people up; they add to the self-worth of others; they build bridges of relationships; they heal; they encourage.

This last word, 'encourage', is worthy of further thought. A word of encouragement makes such a difference. It is true for children. Praise the achievements of a child and you can see the glow which issues in even greater effort. Are we not all children at heart? Our

61

tongues present us with daily opportunities to participate in a ministry of encouragement.

I have discovered something in my ministry as a bishop. Letters of complaint far outnumber those of appreciation or thanks. So often it is the good things that go unsung. If this represents human nature, then it is human nature unredeemed. It forces us to ask whether we are with the nine healed lepers who went their way or the one who returned to thank Jesus.

Gracious words come from a heart of grace. It is a gift worth cultivating.

PRAYER
Lord, help me so to realize the effect of what I say to others that I may truly desire the gift of gracious speech. May my words be sacramental, the outward expression of your inner gift of grace.

RESOLUTION
To find a strength in other people before a weakness; to speak in appreciation before condemnation; to participate today in the ministry of encouragement.

No Tongue

Then they brought to him [Jesus] a demoniac who was blind and mute. (Matt. 12.22)

REFLECTION

Some people who read this book may lack the power of speech because of a congenital condition or through a stroke, or other cause.

Those of us who can speak can only dimly imagine what it is like to travel through life unable to put one's thoughts, desires and feelings into words. Other means of communication are available — the written word, the computer printout, signs and symbols — but none is so immediate, so subtle, so precise as speech.

The nearest experience I can get is being in another country and not being able to speak the language. I point at the bananas on the fruit barrow and hold up the requisite number of fingers. I go to the supermarket where I can put my choices into a basket, rather than face the ordeal of personal service. I do not know how to tell the taxi driver to take me to the airport.

I recall an incident in Milan. The taxi driver with whom I could hold no conversation was whistling. I recognized the tune and sang, in English, 'I'm dreaming of a white Christmas', and said the name, 'Bing Crosby'. He grasped my arm firmly and warmly. We had something in common. We had communicated.

Without speech I could not say, 'please', 'thank you' or 'I love you'. I could not join in the corporate prayers of the Church. I could not sing. I could not read a bedtime story to the children. You will be able to make your own list of the blessings of speech.

There is something else here, however. Without speech people can be isolated, cut off, ignored. How do we react in the presence of those who have a speech disability? Do we distance ourselves in embarrassment or flee the scene altogether? Do we treat such persons as lacking in intelligence, subhuman in some way? In what non-verbal ways can we communicate our welcome, our care, our concern, at the same time being receptive to the unspoken needs and concerns of other people?

PRAYER
Father, we who have a speech impairment ask not for patronizing pity but for acceptance, recognition, inclusion. We thank you for all those who take the time and trouble to listen to our unspoken thoughts, ideas, needs and aspirations. May we always be treated as truly and fully human, just as your Son always treated others.

RESOLUTION
To 'tune in' each day to the unspoken, but not unexpressed, messages which others seek to communicate.

Witnessing Tongue

[Jesus] said . . . , 'Go home to your friends, and tell them how much the Lord has done for you, and what mercy he has shown you.' (Mark 5.19)

REFLECTION

There have been many definitions of evangelism. I like this one, 'Evangelism is a sharing of gladness.'

I fall in love and I want all my friends to know about it; I want them to meet this wonderful person in my life. I share the gladness by telling others. I think it shows or glows in my life as well.

So it is with our witnessing to others of our love for God and our trust in him. Our joyful discovery of life in all its fullness will be communicated through our speech as well as wordlessly through the manner, the quality, the peacefulness and contentedness of our lives.

These two things, what we say and how we live, go together. Words alone will not do. Indeed the words we utter can be right but effectively negated by the contradiction of our lives. Remember the saying, 'I can't hear what you are saying. What you are speaks so loudly.' Evangelism will bear fruit only where the speaking and the living are of matching quality.

Many of us are only just discovering the use of our tongues in witness. Our religion has often been internalized, personalized, privatized. Yet daily life presents us with opportunities to speak naturally and sensitively of what God means to us. Every day may bring an opportunity to share our gladness.

65

What part does your tongue play in witnessing to Christ? Is your tongue silent? Does it on the other hand intrude insensitively? Does it wait to sense the right moment, the receptive moment, God's moment? Does it know when to stop?

If our examination of the 'witnessing' tongue shows that it never speaks to non-Church friends of the faith that is within us, we are hoarding the treasure and keeping it for ourselves.

Notice the Lord's timeless command in today's text!

PRAYER
Lord, teach me how to speak simply and naturally of you, and enable me to discern when it is right to speak and when it is right to wait. So may my tongue become your agent of evangelism in a world of unbelief.

RESOLUTION
To share the gladness of the gospel with others as the opportunity is given.

Christ's Tongue

Truly I tell you . . . Heaven and earth will pass away,
but my words will not pass away. (Matt. 24.34–5)

REFLECTION

> O let me hear thee speaking
> In accents clear and still.
>
> *(J.E. Bode)*

Not all of the words uttered by the tongue of Christ were beautiful. Some of them were hard; some of them were challenging.

There is beauty in, 'Come to me, all you that are weary and are carrying heavy burdens, and I will give you rest.' (Matt. 11.28) What other beautiful sayings of Jesus can you recall?

On the other hand we are not so comfortable with, 'Do not think that I have come to bring peace to the earth; I have not come to bring peace, but a sword. For I have come to set a man against his father, and a daughter against her mother.' (Matt. 10.34–5) Recall some other hard words from the tongue of Jesus.

There is challenge in, 'If any want to become my followers, let them deny themselves and take up their cross and follow me.' (Matt. 16.24) What other challenges did Jesus make? Certainly as we read the Gospels, we can hear Christ speaking 'in accents clear and still'. The words have a value, a meaning and an authority because they come from his tongue.

But words need to resound with a present application and not merely come to us from the past. We need to discover the point of intersection between his story and our own personal story.

Take, for example, the death of Jesus. In the agony, in the dying and in the death of Jesus, I am there; you are there. Your story, your grief, your despair, your death, your experience are drawn together at the cross with Christ's experience.

A relationship comes to an end. Once it meant a lot to you but it is over. Part of you dies. Someone you trusted turns against you. You feel betrayed. The news is bad, the prognosis grim. You have been out of work so long you forget what it is to experience the dignity of earning your way in life. The handouts are killing you. Someone you love dies; even through the numbness you feel the pain. Even now I have not told your story. But Jesus has. He tells it in the desolation and abandonment and suffering and pain of the cross. His story and your story meet. He puts you in the picture. The words of Christ come alive as we allow his story and our story to intersect.

PRAYER
Lord Jesus, I thank you for your words and for their eternal significance. May I so listen to your words that they intersect with my life here and now. Out of that cross of intersection bring new life to me; for your name's sake.

RESOLUTION
To speak to myself each day words which have come from the tongue of Jesus and to turn those words into prayer.

FOR GROUP DISCUSSION *OR*
INDIVIDUAL REFLECTION

1. What is the difference between 'jolliness' or *'bonhomie'* and 'praise'? What provision is there in the worship of your parish for a sense of awe and wonder in the presence of God?

2. How can the fellowship, ministry and worship of the Church be made accessible to those who have a speech impairment? How can we be open to their ministry to us?

3. How effective are we in speaking to our non-Christian friends about our faith in Christ? What inhibits us? How can we be assisted to do this naturally and sensitively?

4. Share your favourite words of beauty and encouragement from the tongue of Jesus. Then remind one another of his hard and challenging sayings. How do we handle his uncomfortable words?

Our Ears

SUNDAY (LENT 5) · DAY 33

Listening Ears

We must pay greater attention to what we have heard, so that we do not drift away from it. (Heb. 2.1)

REFLECTION

'If we knew how to listen to God, we should hear him speaking to us, for God does speak. He speaks in his gospel; he speaks also through life — that new gospel to which we ourselves add a page each day.' (Michel Quoist)

Years ago I received valuable advice from an old and wise priest. I was trying to deal with the problem of wandering thoughts during worship. I sometimes came away from worship with nothing lodged in my head even though several passages of Scripture had been read. Two things he said to me: first, come expectant; come expecting that God has something to communicate to you. Second, look for one thing. Let the rest go, at least for the time being; latch on to the one thing, and chew on it. Be ready to listen to God.

So much depends upon our expectant, listening ears. It is our ears that provide the basis for this week's reflections.

Our God is one who moves out from himself towards us, seeking us, wanting to communicate with us. Through an attitude of expectancy we open ourselves up to him, meeting him part-way. God speaks to us through life, as Michel Quoist reminds us. God is not confined to a book, even to his book. He is a participant in life, not a spectator. He is alongside us, walking with us, talking to us. Part of our prayer time can be used for reflecting on our day-to-day lives, listening for him with his word of illumination, comfort, warning or encouragement.

Often enough in our lives we experience brokenness. It may be disappointment in love, early redundancy, with loss of work and status, the death of a loved one, a life-threatening situation. The God of the cross knows about brokenness. He speaks to us, not from some vantage point outside and above us. He speaks from within the brokenness, as one who shares it.

He speaks, too, if we have ears to hear, from within our joys. He knows about light after darkness, sunshine after tears, peace after strife, life after death.

We can hear him in the Scriptures. We can hear him in the words of others. We can hear him in the events of our lives. We can hear him in the recesses of our hearts and minds.

PRAYER
Lord God, I often act as though you are a God of past actions and past words. Help me to tune into your overtures here and now.

RESOLUTION
To make room in my daily prayer time for more listening.

Blocked Ears

If you close your ear to the cry of the poor, you will cry out and not be heard. (Prov. 21.13)

REFLECTION

An old saying runs, 'There are none so deaf as those who do not want to hear.' It is our eyes that are fitted with lids. But we can be just as selective with our ears. There are some things which we do not want to hear.

How selective are you with regard to what you hear and heed?

People now speak of 'compassion fatigue'. There are so many voices crying for our assistance that we react by rejecting them all. It is a form of blockage in the ear which effectively cuts off entry to the heart.

Are your ears blocked?

What about those who are nearest to you — spouse, family, close friends? Do you really listen?

What are they trying to say to you? They need you to listen to them — to take in their cries.

I may well be more available to the demands of the telephone than I am to those with whom I live. Perhaps you have heard of the person who, to ensure being heard, resorted to writing an appointment in their spouse's diary!

There are the voices of those in the nearer as well as the wider community — the cries of those who sleep out at night, the voices of the world's parents who have to watch their children starve to death. Out of every flood, fire, famine, cyclone come to our ears the cries of people in need. Are your ears open or blocked?

When the religious leaders saw the beaten-up figure by the side of the road, they turned their heads and passed by on the other side. Do we ever use our ears selectively to enable us to 'pass by on the other side'?

PRAYER
Lord God, unblock the channels of communication so that the messages that come to my ears may be passed on to my heart, and relayed in turn to my will and to my hands; I ask it through the one who is always alert to the cries of your people, Jesus Christ.

RESOLUTION
To do more than hear — to listen, to heed — to act according to the demands of love.

Responsive Ears

Be doers of the word, and not merely hearers. (Jas. 1.22)

REFLECTION

The newly appointed incumbent caused something of a stir. The vicar preached exactly the same sermon on each of the first three Sundays immediately following the induction. Parishioners were perturbed. The churchwardens confronted the vicar. To their expressions of concern the priest responded, 'I know that I have repeated the same sermon but you have not done the first one yet!'

Somehow the preacher had the idea that actions would stem from hearing. We hear a lot of words in church — two or three readings from the Scriptures, the Psalm and the sermon. What happens to these words? What do our ears do with them?

Do we listen, expecting to hear a word for us? What difference does it make that the Word has been read and preached? To what extent does the message received by our ears modify, change, transform, stimulate, fashion our actions?

St Paul tells us that 'a person is justified by faith apart from works prescribed by the law'. (Rom. 3.28) A right relationship with God is the result of the free gift of his love. We cannot merit it. We cannot earn it through our good works. But faith and works need to be seen as partners. The fruit of faith shows in the quality of daily life. 'Faith by itself, if it has no works, is dead.' (Jas. 2.17)

At the end of the Holy Communion service we are dismissed with the words, 'Go in peace to love and serve the Lord.' The implication is that God has commissioned us to return to the world as doers of the words which we have heard with our ears.

What did you hear last Sunday? Have you done it?

PRAYER
Lord, may your grace in my life bear fruit through my deeds, not for the recognition and praise of me, but to your greater honour and glory.

RESOLUTION
To ensure that action flows from the hearing, the reading and the preaching of the Word on Sundays.

Attentive Ears

Let everyone be quick to listen, slow to speak. (Jas. 1.19)

REFLECTION

We are given two ears and one tongue. The message is clear. We are to do a lot more listening than speaking.

An important pastoral principle is to be found in the words, 'You don't have to do anything, you just have to be there.' Christian ministry is not having all the answers. It is not about providing solutions to everyone else's problems and questions.

In the early days of my ministry I did not understand that. I felt inadequate when people came to seek my help. They would tell me their story, share their hurt, put their concerns out in front of them. I could not see the solutions.

Then I learned a very important truth. We may have some experience to share, some insights to communicate. But the most important thing is to listen — to show that we care by listening, making enough 'noises' to encourage the other person to empty out in an atmosphere of acceptance and confidentiality. We *may* have an inspired utterance to make but a big part of the healing is in the sharing, in the verbalizing.

A listening ministry is one which most of us can undertake. Someone trusts us. They are hurt, perplexed, anxious, distraught. Accept the trust; show that you care; hold back the words, the judgements, the advice — and listen.

Today we think about the ministry of our ears. There is a gift of listening, an art of listening, a ministry of listening. 'You do not have to do anything, you just have to be there.'

Being there for others with our ears wide open — are we exercising that ministry?

PRAYER
Lord, make me quick to listen and slow to speak, a trustworthy confidant with a ministry of hearing; for Jesus' sake.

RESOLUTION
To be available each day as an empty vessel for those who need to pour out their griefs and troubles.

No Ears

They brought to him [Jesus] a deaf man who had an impediment in his speech. (Mark 7.32)

REFLECTION
What if? What if:

I could no longer hear my favourite song?

I could not hear the voice of those I love?

I could not hear the rain on the roof, the laughter of children, the words of Scripture, the prayers of the faithful, the birds in the trees, the cicadas in the bush, the lowing of cattle, the wind in the trees, the surf on the beach, the crackling fire, the bubbling brook, the cathedral bells?

I lived in a world of silence?

You may care to list for yourself the sounds that mean so much to you. Actually write them down.

Each of our senses is a great gift. Our hearing is precious. It requires protecting from the assaults of modern life. We need to give thanks for our ears.

There are those who cannot hear. Perhaps some who read this have not ever been able to hear or have been going deaf for some time. It is strange how we treat people who are hard of hearing. They are so annoying! We resort to shouting; we get cross. So the person with a hearing disability suffers twice over: the disability itself, and then the shouting. We can even treat the hard of hearing as though they were stupid.

How do you treat such people? How does the Church provide for such people? Is there a hearing aid loop in your parish church? If not, why not? Can someone 'sign' the words of the service?

The deeper question is, what place do the deaf and hard of hearing have in the community of the Church?

PRAYER

Creator God, I thank you for the gift of hearing and for all the beautiful sounds that abound in life. Save me from offering pity; help me to extend compassion and to ensure the dignity of those whose gift of hearing is impaired; in the name of Christ, I pray.

RESOLUTION

To learn from the deaf and hard of hearing and to accept their ministry to me.

The Inescapable God

O Lord, you have searched me and known me. You know when I sit down and when I rise up; you discern my thoughts from far away. You search out my path and my lying down, and are acquainted with all my ways. Even before a word is on my tongue, O Lord, you know it completely. (Ps. 139.1–4)

REFLECTION

'The remarkable thing about the way in which people talk about God, or about their relation to God, is that it seems to escape them completely that God hears what they are saying.' (Søren Kierkegaard)

God has ears!

The doctrine of the omniscience of God tells us that God knows all. The omnipresence of God means that God is always present at every point of time and space and eternity. This means that God hears all. Whatever we say, wherever we say it, God is aware. 'Even before a word is on my tongue, O Lord, you know it completely.'

Do we really believe that? It is easy to give a 'head' answer to a proposition about the nature of God. The real test comes when we consider how that truth touches our lives. God hears all we say. Yet we may treat him as largely absent, available to be summoned up at our initiative.

The truth is he hears my words of thanks and appreciation; he hears my silence when I take things for granted. He hears my hymns of praise and thanksgiving; he hears my muttered grizzles and complaints. He knows of my truth, openness and honesty as well as of my deceit, hypocrisy and dishonesty. He observes my encouragement of others, and sees my condemnation and put down. What I say *to* people and *about* people are equally before him.

My public statements and private conversations are both known to him. I speak up, even though it is personally costly, or I bite my tongue and let an injustice go unchallenged. God knows. The question for our self-examination is, what messages is God receiving from us? What falls upon his ears?

One of the lessons of Advent is that in view of the promised return of God in judgement, we should live each day as if it were our last. The same may be applied to what God hears us say. What if the words we have just said were our last? What if we were to be judged by them?

PRAYER
Father, because you hear all, you know my worst words as well as my best. Reform not only my speech but the inner movements of my spirit, until they conform to the words and life of your Son.

RESOLUTION
To recognize God as the unseen listener to everything I say.

Christ's Ears

He is able . . . to save those who approach God through him, since he always lives to make intercession for them. (Heb. 7.25)

REFLECTION

Today we think about the things which came to the ears of Christ. They have an application to our own lives.

At the beginning of his ministry, he heard the announcement of John the Baptist, 'Here is the Lamb of God who takes away the sin of the world.' Jesus, Lamb of God, have mercy on me, take away my sins.

At his baptism he heard the voice of approval, 'This is my Son, the Beloved, with whom I am well pleased.' I too am God's son — God's daughter — twice over! I am his child by creation; I am his child by redemption. What aspects of my life are pleasing to God? What are not?

Christ heard the plea of the centurion, 'Lord, my servant is lying at home paralysed, in terrible distress.' For whom am I responsible to pray? Who are the people I should bring to Christ for healing?

On the storm-swept sea Christ was woken with the shout, 'Lord, save us! We are perishing.' Without his saving action we all perish. What are the storms around me? Lord, give me peace within and without.

Christ knew the sting of criticism, 'Why does your teacher eat with tax collectors and sinners?' Am I more concerned for my reputation than I am for the communication of the gospel?

He knew the need of the disciples for understanding. 'Explain to us the parable of the weeds of the field', he heard them say. Am I ready to ask? Ready to listen? Am I an enquiring, teachable spirit?

Asked by Peter about the extent of forgiveness, Christ answered that seventy-seven times not seven times was the requirement. Sometimes I have not even forgiven once. What grudges do I carry with me?

He heard the young man's query, 'What good deed must I do to have eternal life?' Christ's reply went to the heart of the matter for that person. What is my particular richness, my obstacle, my danger, my obsession, my preoccupation, my priority?

He heard the quarrel about greatness. He stooped and washed their feet. What recognition, status, power do I hunger for?

There are many more things that came to the ears of Christ. Take one of the Gospels. Read it right through. Note the things that came to the ears of Jesus and how he responded. Apply that response to your own life.

Christ knows you; he hears you; he responds to you.

PRAYER
Lord Christ, you not only hear me and respond to me, but you make intercession for me. I thank you that I can pray 'through Jesus Christ who is Lord'.

RESOLUTION
To bring to the ears of Christ each day my ACTS of prayer – Adoration, Confession, Thanksgiving, Supplication.

FOR GROUP DISCUSSION *OR*
INDIVIDUAL REFLECTION

1. Is our Sunday worship an escape from the cries of the real world or a pause for refreshment and preparation which sends us back to attend to those cries?

2. What does it mean to pray 'through Jesus Christ our Lord'?

3. What provision does your parish church make for those who have difficulty in hearing? What else can be done about it? What gifts and ministry can the hearing impaired offer to the Church?

4. Share with one another your experiences of the ministry of listening. How can we become more effective listeners?

Christs Body

~~~~~~

What Jesus Said (1)

My Father, if it is possible, let this cup pass from me; yet not what I want but what you want. (Matt. 26.39)

REFLECTION

'God is the master of the scenes; we must not choose what part we shall act; it concerns us only to be careful that we do it well, always saying, "If this please God, let it be as it is." ' (Jeremy Taylor)

It is proper for us in Holy Week to attend to the tongue and eyes and ears of Jesus, reflecting on what he said and saw and heard on his journey to the cross. The things which he spoke at that time are unforgettable. All of them merit our attention. We must make a choice.

So today we are with him in the Garden of Gethsemane. Darkness is gathering around him. The betrayal, arrest and trial are imminent. It is to prayer that Jesus resorts. If only we could pray like this.

'My Father': this is not the corporate 'our Father' of the Lord's Prayer. The pronoun is singular, personal, intimate. Father and Son are bound by love. The Garden of Gethsemane becomes a private chapel, Jesus' place of retreat. There he communes with the one who sent him.

'If it is possible': are not all things possible to God? But God cannot act contrary to his own nature. He cannot be other than loving. 'If it is possible, and still be in accord with your nature and purpose, let this cup pass from me.' If this constitutes a limitation placed on God, then Jesus accepts it.

'Let this cup pass from me': Jesus is human. He does not want to suffer and die. He does not want to drink the cup to its bitter dregs. Shades of the struggle with temptation in the wilderness are apparent: 'If you are the Son of God . . . command these stones to become loaves of bread . . . throw yourself down . . . fall down and worship me.' Is there not another way? An easier way? The prayer is costly. Great drops of sweat, like blood, fall to the ground.

'Yet not what I want but what you want': their wills meet, converge, coalesce. As the love of Father and Son is one love, so the will of Father and Son is one will. His ministry had begun with the defeat of temptation, 'One does not live by bread alone . . . Do not put the Lord your God to the test . . . Worship the Lord your God, and serve only him.' His life is drawing to its close marked by the same triumph over temptation.

When we pray each day, 'Your will be done', what is the cost? Where do our wills and the divine will meet, coalesce?

PRAYER
'O Saviour of the world, who by thy cross and precious blood hast redeemed us, save us and help us, we humbly beseech thee, O Lord.' (*Book of Common Prayer*)

RESOLUTION
To find my Garden of Gethsemane so that when I pray, 'Your will be done', it will be a reality.

What Jesus Said (2)

Father, forgive them; for they do not know what they are doing. (Luke 23.34)

REFLECTION

'Nothing in this lost world bears the impress of the Son of God so surely as forgiveness.' (Alice Cary)

The words of Jesus stem from the inner nature of Jesus. It is of his very nature to forgive. So he utters his prayer of forgiveness. We are not told exactly when, but for some reason I have always thought that it was as the nails were driven in. Most people would have shrieked and cursed; some would have lost consciousness; some would have been gripped by the silence of terror: but Jesus speaks a prayer for his persecutors.

'Father, forgive them': he means those who are doing the deed, even if they are merely obeying orders. But 'them' must surely include Judas who betrayed him, his enemies who engineered it all, as well as Pilate and those who, denying him justice, found the guiltless guilty.

'They do not know what they are doing': Judas did not know what his treachery would lead to. His enemies did not know that Jesus was the anointed of God. Pilate did not know the truth when it stood personified before him. The soldiers did not know they were killing God's Son. Jesus makes excuses for them all. He pleads extenuating circumstances. These words of Jesus bring to us the very purpose of Christ's death. 'He died that we might be forgiven.' They express his continuing role on our behalf. He died once for all. He pleads that saving death continually.

He is our advocate. We are the accused. We call him to our side to speak for us. He represents us, pleads our cause, seeks our forgiveness in the courts of heaven. 'Father, forgive them . . .'

He is our mediator. He comes between the two parties, God and us, as reconciler. Christ, the mediator, reconciles us to the Father. 'Father, forgive them . . .'

'He is the one who ever lives to make intercession for us.' It is only through Christ that we have access to the Father. 'Father, forgive them . . .'

Even now, faced by our daily unfaithfulness, weakness, betrayal, wickedness, he prays, 'Father, forgive them, for they do not know what they are doing.'

PRAYER
'O Saviour of the world, who by thy cross and precious blood hast redeemed us, save us and help us, we humbly beseech thee, O Lord.' (*Book of Common Prayer*)

RESOLUTION
To name before God those whom I have not forgiven, and to seek the grace I need to forgive even the unforgivable.

Where Jesus Trod

So they took Jesus; and carrying the cross by himself, he went out to what is called The Place of the Skull. (John 19.16–17)

REFLECTION

> To mock your reign, O dearest Lord,
> they made a crown of thorns;
> set you with taunts along the road
> from which no man returns.
>
> *(F. Pratt-Green)*

The route which Jesus took for his journey to the cross is sometimes called the 'Via Dolorosa'. It took him from the judgement hall of Pilate, where he was condemned to death, to Calvary, the mountain where he was crucified.

We thoughtlessly sing, 'O let me see your footmarks and in them plant my own.' Shall we apply these words to this last journey? Will we take up *our* cross and follow him? It is his journey *with* the cross, *to* the cross. At least in our imaginations we might try a few steps with him.

It was a long route through the busiest streets, a warning to those who might contemplate crime. Jesus is forced to carry the cross alone. This cross-bearer is our God. He bears the load of human hatred, rejection, and cruelty.

Under the weight his feet stumble. He falls. Simon of Cyrene is pressed into service. If we would be his disciples, we must take up our cross daily and, carrying it, follow him. Behind Jesus came a band of women weeping for him. He seems to rebuke them. 'Weep not for me, but for yourselves.' Days of terror are coming. But perhaps they are words of consolation. He is thinking of them. He calls for their repentance, not their sympathy. We too might weep for him. Better, he says, to weep for our sins and to be sorry.

His feet bring him at length to Calvary. They dress him as a king. They hit him. They spit at him. They mock him. Then they strip him again of all his clothes. It is a sign. He is giving up everything for us.

We come to the last terrible scene. Even nature cannot bear what is happening. Darkness descends. The walk is over. The feet are still. Jesus is crucified. He has gone the whole way. There is no limit to God's love.

PRAYER
'O Saviour of the world, who by thy cross and precious blood hast redeemed us, save us and help us, we humbly beseech thee, O Lord.' (*Book of Common Prayer*)

RESOLUTION
To stop complaining and to ask for strength to struggle after Christ.

What Jesus Saw

When Jesus saw his mother and the disciple whom he loved standing beside her, he said . . . 'Woman, here is your son . . . Here is your mother.' (John 19.26–7)

REFLECTION

> They crucified him on Calvary,
> Upon an April day;
> And because he had been her little son
> She followed him all the way.
>
> *(Hilaire Belloc)*

It took a long time to die on a cross. Breathing was difficult. Pain came in waves. The eyes of Jesus took in the whole scene — the curious crowd, the mockers, the soldiers. There was hardly a familiar face among them. Could no one watch with him one brief hour? Then he saw her. His eyes focused on his mother and the beloved John.

Here was the mother who had borne him. She had nursed him. Mary had helped him to grow in wisdom and in stature and in divine and human favour. For her part she had never forgotten the prophetic words of Simeon as he held the infant Jesus, 'This child is destined for the falling and the rising of many in Israel, and to be a sign that will be opposed . . . and a sword will pierce your own soul too.'

She had had to learn, as all parents must, to let him be himself, to let him fulfil his own destiny, to let him go. Parents can so easily frustrate the God-given vocations of their children.

It had been hard for her. Even at the age of twelve, when Joseph and Mary had anxiously searched for him, he had mildly rebuked them. At other times he had put his followers ahead of the relationships of blood. Sometimes it seemed as though he had renounced the normal relationships of home and family.

This word from the cross precludes such an interpretation. His eyes pick out Mary and John. 'Woman, behold your son.' Then, 'Son, behold your mother.' He sees her loneliness. He sees her grief. He sees her pain. He sees her faithfulness. He sees the sword piercing her heart. In his extremity he provides for her.

Even on the cross, his eyes are for others. Amidst his own suffering, he takes in the needs of others and speaks to them. He looks at you, he has a word for you.

PRAYER
'O Saviour of the world, who by thy cross and precious blood hast redeemed us, save us and help us, we humbly beseech thee, O Lord.' (*Book of Common Prayer*)

RESOLUTION
To see, even through my own pain and tears, the needs of those dearest to me.

What Jesus Did

Jesus took a loaf of bread, and after blessing it he broke it. . . . Then he took a cup, and after giving thanks he gave it to them. (Matt. 26.26–7)

REFLECTION

'If ever I had any doubts about the fundamental realities of religion, they could always be dispelled by one memory — the light upon my father's face as he came back from early communion.' (Alfred Noyes)

What Jesus did on that day before his death has left its mark on Christian worship.

He was at table with the twelve in the upper room. Before him were the most basic items of food and drink — bread and wine. What he did invested those ordinary things forever with new significance.

He took the bread into his hands, he gave thanks, 'he broke it'. He said 'This is my body which is given for you. Do this in remembrance of me.'

Then he took the cup of wine; he gave thanks. He said, 'This is my blood which is shed for you and for many for the forgiveness of sins. Do this, as often as you drink it, in remembrance of me.' Last of all, with his own hands, he gave it to them to eat and drink.

To my mind comes the great painting of the *Last Supper* by Leonardo da Vinci. In it I see the Church gathering with its Lord. In the centre is Christ. All are looking towards him. He is the one who gives purpose, meaning and value to life. Is he at the centre of your daily life as well as at the centre of your Sunday worship?

He is surrounded by his followers, then and now. All eyes are on him. His followers belong together because in the first place they belong to him. Is Christ the source of our unity? Does the Holy Communion help us to experience the relationship of being Christian together? Or does it separate us as 'I make *my* communion'?

He feeds them with broken bread and wine out-poured. To the disciples they were signs of his coming death. To us they are sacrament — effective signs, a means of grace, a window into that saving death. The Holy Communion is not so much our journey back in time as it is that once-for-all saving event made effective here and now.

Read slowly, as if for the first time, the Prayer of Consecration from *The Book of Common Prayer* or Thanksgiving for Holy Communion on page 920 of *The Alternative Service Book*.

PRAYER
'O Saviour of the world, who by thy cross and precious blood hast redeemed us, save us and help us, we humbly beseech thee, O Lord.' (*Book of Common Prayer*)

RESOLUTION
To discern more clearly the Christ who presides at the Holy Communion, and that it is his action in which we participate.

What Jesus Heard

Then Pilate asked, 'Why, what evil has he done?' but they shouted all the more, 'Let him be crucified!' (Matt. 27.23)

REFLECTION
There were many sounds that came to the ears of Jesus on that last day. In his book of the same name, David Owen calls them the *Sounds of the Passion*. We listen to those sounds as we seek to be with Jesus.

He heard the shout of the crowd, 'Away with him! Crucify him!' There was not one friendly voice to speak for him, only the cruel crowd, ignorant no doubt of what they were doing, who condemned him. It is the rejection of the whole of humanity, the sin of the whole world, which he is bearing, the innocent for the guilty.

He heard the thud of the hammer. The carpenter is himself nailed. Crucifixion is a terrible spectacle. No wonder Jesus had prayed, 'Father, save me from this hour.' This is the ultimate test of love for the one who said, 'No one has greater love than this, to lay down one's life for one's friends.'

He heard the rattle of the dice. The soldiers cast lots to see who would receive which part of his garments. Christ dies for the world whilst that very world seeks diversions as an escape from reality.

He heard his own cry of victory, 'It is finished.' It was the most demanding task ever given to any single human being. On the cross Jesus fulfilled it, accomplished it, perfected it, completed it. And what is 'it'? Nothing less than the reconciliation of men and women to God, our redemption. He 'opened the kingdom of heaven to all believers'. The cross is both the pledge of God's love and the sign of his victory.

Not long after this came his last sound, 'Father, into your hands I commend my spirit.' The last words. The last breath.

Kneel at the foot of the cross. Listen to the sounds of the Passion: the shout of the crowd — the weeping of the women — the crowing of the cock — the clatter of Judas' coins — the splash of Pilate's hand-washing — the thud of the hammer — the rattle of the dice — the cry of victory.

PRAYER
'O Saviour of the world, who by thy cross and precious blood hast redeemed us, save us and help us, we humbly beseech thee, O Lord.' (*Book of Common Prayer*)

RESOLUTION
To prepare to renew my baptismal promises on Easter day, so that dying with Christ I might live with him.

The Body Buried

*Now there was a garden in the place where he was
crucified, and in the garden there was a new tomb. . . .
And so . . . they laid Jesus there.* (John 19.41–2)

REFLECTION

At birth Christ was wrapped in swaddling clothes. He
was cradled in the warm arms of his mother. As with
all parents, Mary and Joseph would have wanted to see
that his hands and feet were functioning, his eyes and
ears responding to stimulus, his lungs and voice strong.

At death Christ is wrapped in grave-clothes. He is
alone in the dark tomb. His feet no longer carry him on
his daily ministry. His hands are stilled from blessing.
He speaks no longer. His ears receive no sounds. His
eyes are closed forever.

> Lifeless lies the pierced body,
> Resting in its rocky bed.
> (*W.D. MacLagan*)

Death is one of the forbidden subjects of our age, but
some day our bodies too will have finished their earthly
course. When we grieve for another we are in part grieving for ourselves. We mourn at Christ's death and burial. We identify with him — Christ in us, we in Christ.

Today we reflect on Christ's death and on our mor-
tality. Pause for this reflection before moving on.
Christ is dead and it seems God is doing nothing about
it! From the outside, beyond the sealed entrance,
nothing is happening. Nothing *can* happen. It is all
over.

There are times in all our lives when we reach the absolute limit. We are engulfed by crisis and disaster. We pray. Nothing seems to happen. God is ignoring us. He is deaf to us. Those experiences, those days, are our Holy Saturdays, days of waiting and weeping.

Yet in the stillness God is. In the silence God is working out his will and purpose. He does not abandon us, any more than he abandoned Christ at his death and burial.

Beneath the soil, unseen and unheard, the buried seed, filled with the creativity of God, is already beginning its journey to the light.

PRAYER

Soul of Christ, sanctify me.
Body of Christ, save me.
Blood of Christ, invigorate me.
Water from the side of Christ, wash me.
Passion of Christ, strengthen me.
O God Jesu, hear me.
Within thy wounds hide me.

Suffer me not to be separated from thee.
From the malicious enemy defend me.
In the hour of my death call me,
And bid me come to thee.
That with thy saints I may praise thee.
For ever and ever.

(*Anima Christi*)

RESOLUTION

To seek that patience which accepts God's timing and God's way.

The Body Risen

. . . Jesus came and stood among them and said, 'Peace be with you.' After he said this, he showed them his hands and his side. Then the disciples rejoiced when they saw the Lord. (John 20.19–20)

REFLECTION

The earthly mission of Jesus had ended in disaster. That is how his followers felt.

Then came Easter Day. The stone at the entrance was rolled away. The tomb was empty, the body gone. By itself the empty tomb suggests that the body was stolen or that Jesus had not died, but had merely swooned and later recovered.

But the absence of the body was followed by the appearances of Jesus. For Easter is not the commemoration of an empty tomb; it is the celebration of a Risen Christ. He appeared. They recognized him. They knew the face.

The voice was familiar. The final authentication was the wounded hands and scarred side. In some way things were different. He seemed to appear when and where he wished, no longer anchored in time and space. But it was his body all right, gloriously free. Even Thomas was satisfied without actually touching Jesus as he had earlier demanded. The risen body of Christ evoked his faith in awe and adoration, 'My Lord and my God.'

The resurrection of Jesus is something to shout about. The whole meaning and value and purpose of our lives is at once vastly expanded. It was the resurrection which changed depressed disciples into eager apostles, which accounts for Sunday as our day of worship, which gave birth to the Christian Church and its mission to the world.

Christmas is merely another birth, Good Friday another wasteful death, the Holy Communion a charade unless it is true that the one who died is the one who rose again.

In the Apostles' Creed we affirm our belief in 'the resurrection of the body'. Nowhere does the immortality of the soul become an article of faith. For life which transcends death is God's gift, not the result of having an immortal soul. We shall be given a body of a new order suited to the new life, yet with continuity of identity. The resurrection of the body means not the reassembling of the particles of the dead body, for flesh and blood cannot inherit the Kingdom of God. Rather we shall be raised in a way which retains our individual personality. We shall recognize and be recognized.

Resurrection life is not the denial of all that has gone before, but the fulfilment of it. Perhaps it is only then that we shall appreciate fully what Jesus meant when he said, 'I came that they may have life, and have it abundantly.'

PRAYER
Risen Lord, I am yours; I am marked with the sign of your cross; in baptism I died with you and rose with you; help me to live now the resurrection life which is the fruit of your endless love for me.

RESOLUTION
To walk each day in the company of the Risen Lord.

FOR GROUP DISCUSSION *OR* INDIVIDUAL REFLECTION

1. What is the difference between forgiving and forgetting? Is there anything which we find totally unforgivable? Share with others who and what you find difficult to forgive.

2. Consider these verses from the hymn 'O Jesus I have promised':

    1.
    O Jesus, I have promised
    to serve you to the end;
    Lord, be for ever near me,
    my master and my friend:
    I shall not fear the battle
    if you are by my side,
    nor wander from the pathway
    if you will be my guide

    5.
    Lord, let me see your footmarks
    and in them plant my own;
    that I may follow boldly
    and in your strength alone:
    O guide me, call me, draw me,
    uphold me to the end;
    and then in heaven receive me,
    my Saviour and my friend.
                        (*J.E. Bode*)

Verse 1: What did we promise? When? What is meant by the battle? How are we guided?

Verse 5: How do we place our feet in Christ's foot-marks? What should this mean in our daily lives?

3. Share with one another your understanding of the words of Jesus: 'This is my body . . . This is my blood . . . Do this in remembrance of me.'

4. Read the account of the Emmaus walk and the Risen Christ's appearance in Luke 24.13–35. Discuss together: Why didn't they recognize Jesus? What was it that eventually 'opened their eyes'? Read these verses from *An Australian Prayer Book*:

> As watchmen look for the morning
> So we wait eagerly for you, O Lord.
> Come with the dawning of the day
> and make yourself known to us in the breaking of the bread,
> for you are our God for ever and ever. Amen.

What do the words of the fourth line mean?